## How do you like ou

We would really appreciate you leavi

## Other Picture Books:

For other fun Picture Books by Kampelstone,
simply search for:

Kampelstone Picture Books

Copyright© 2020 by Kampelstone. All rights reserved.
This book or any portion thereof may not be reproduced or used in any manner whatsoever without the express written permission of the publisher.

# FACTS ABOUT ROME

- Rome was founded in 735 BCE by Romulus. Legend says that Romulus and his twin brother Remus were raised by a wolf after being abandoned in the Tiber river. A shepherd discovered the boys and took them in as his own.

- In Rome, there is a law that states that cats are allowed to live wherever they were born. One can see wild cats hanging out nearly everywhere amongst the ruins; in the Colosseum, the Forum, etc

- In Ancient Rome, people loved eating so much that once they were full, they would often vomit to empty their stomachs in order to continue eating.

- As a sign that a person was a citizen in Rome, men wore togas to indicate their status as citizens. Women wore a similar item called a stola but it was not worn to indicate status of citizenship, but to indicate the woman was married.

- Approximately three thousand euros are gathered up from the bottom of the Trevi Fountain every night. The money is donated to a Caritas, a catholic charity which uses the money to help needy families in Rome.

- Throughout the history of battles within the Colosseum, over half a million people and one million wild animals were killed. The last gladiator fight took place in 435 CE.

- Contrary to popular belief, Roman gladiators rarely fought to the death. Instead they were considered celebrities.

- The Roman Emperor Gaius Caesar 'Caligula', third emperor of Rome, is recorded as being an insane tyrant. At one game in the Colosseum, he was bored and ordered that a section of the audience be thrown into the ring to be devoured by wild beasts. He hel conversation with the moon, he appointed his horse as a priest, had sex with his three sisters and turned his palace into a brothel.

- In ancient Rome, Flamingo tongues were considered a popular delicacy.

- Nero, the fifth The ancient Roman Emperor who ruled from 54 – 68 CE is notorious for supposedly singing and playing the fiddle while Rome burned during the Great Fire of Rome. This is in part a fiction since the fiddle was not invented until over a thousand years later. He is however, recorded as singing 'The Sack of Ilium' while the city was burning.

- Rome has 50 monumental fountains and more than a thousand other fountains throughout the city; more than any other city in the world.

- There are nine hundred churches in Rome.

- The symbol SPQR, which is found on monuments and places throughout Rome, stands for "Senatus Populusque Romanus" which means, "The senate and the people of Rome". It is an emblematic abbreviated phrase referring to the government of the Roman Republic.

- Women loved to dye their hair different colors such as red, blonde, orange and even blue. The wealthy wore colored wigs. They dyed their hair using goat fat, bleach, henna, saffron or beech wood ashes.

- The Roman Emperor Trajan built the first ever shopping mall. It contained multiple levels and over 150 outlets that sold everything ranging from food to clothes.

- Trajan's Market is a large complex of ruins that is considered to be the first ever shopping mall. It was built in 100 CE by Apollodorus of Damascus, Trajan's favorite architect.

- When a woman in ancient Rome was having trouble having a child, the doctor would prescribe gladiator blood to increase fertility. Gladiator Blood was used for a number of other medical problems in ancient Rome.

- Before toilet paper was invented, the ancient Romans used a wet sponge and running water in public restrooms.

- Rome was the first city to have a population of one million people.

- The building of the Colosseum was begun by Emperor Vespasian in 70 CE and finished by Titus, his successor. It was built for the people's entertainment, and when it was first opening, there was a 100-day celebration.

Printed in Great Britain
by Amazon